Avoid being a Second World War Evacuee!

'We'll eat again'

Written by
Simon Smith

Illustrated by
David Antram

Created and designed by
David Salariya

The Danger Zone

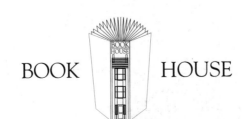

BOOK HOUSE

Contents

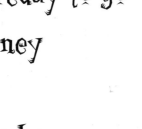
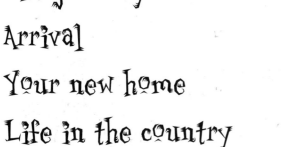

011

Author:

Simon Smith studied history at York University, specialising in twentieth-century history. He is currently Head of History at a senior school and lives in West Sussex with his wife and son.

Artist:

David Antram was born in Brighton, England, in 1958. He studied at Eastbourne College of Art and then worked in advertising for fifteen years before becoming a full-time artist. He has illustrated many children's non-fiction books.

Series creator:

David Salariya was born in Dundee, Scotland. He has illustrated a wide range of books and has created and designed many new series for publishers both in the UK and overseas. In 1989, he established The Salariya Book Company. He lives in Brighton with his wife, illustrator Shirley Willis, and their son Jonathan.

Series editor:
Karen Barker Smith

Editor:
Penny Clarke

Published in Great Britain in 2003 by
Book House, an imprint of
The Salariya Book Company Ltd
25 Marlborough Place, Brighton BN1 1UB

Please visit the Salariya Book Company at:
www.salariya.com
www.book-house.co.uk

ISBN 1 904194 82 6

A catalogue record
for this book is available
from the British Library.

Printed and bound in Belgium.

Printed on paper
from sustainable forests.

The Beano is (TM) and
© D.C. Thomson & Co., Ltd.

SPAM is a registered trademark
of Hormel Foods Corporation
for chopped pork and ham.

Introduction

You are a 10-year-old girl who lives in London with your family. It is September 1939 and the threat of war in Europe has been hanging over the whole country. Germany has just invaded Poland and so Britain has declared war on Germany to help defend Poland. That will mean danger from German attack, especially for anyone living in large British cities, because Germany has threatened to attack them by air. London is in particular danger. Not only is it the capital city, it is in the south-east of the country and so within easy range of German bombers. It is a time of great danger for everyone, including you and your family.

To protect you and other children living in London and the south-east, the government has decided to evacuate you. Instead of continuing to live in German target areas, you will be sent to the countryside where you will be safer (or so they say!). However, this will be no holiday, it will be a journey into the unknown without your family. And even if you've sometimes wished you were a million miles away from them, this separation is for real – and you'd give almost anything not to go!

War is approaching

Peace in our time?

Neville Chamberlain

CHAMBERLAIN AND HITLER. The British Prime Minister, Neville Chamberlain (above), fears that the German Führer, Adolf Hitler (below), wants revenge because Germany lost the First World War. Chamberlain hopes his policy of appeasement will help avoid war and so give 'Peace in our time'.

It is September 1938. Adolf Hitler has taken over some of Czechoslovakia's land. Britain and France promise to help the Czechs. This could lead to war, but Neville Chamberlain is trying to keep the peace. As you walk around London you see barrage balloons in the sky, sandbags around buildings and air-raid shelters being made in parks and gardens. Everyone has a gas mask to protect them if there are poison gas attacks like those in the First World War. Your gas mask is uncomfortable and makes the air taste funny. Everyone carries their masks with them in cardboard containers.

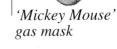

'Mickey Mouse' gas mask

GAS MASKS. The gas masks the government has given to adults are too big for babies and young children. So they issue smaller and more appealing 'Mickey Mouse' gas masks for toddlers and respirators for babies.

Baby respirator

Adolf Hitler

The bomber

A t a meeting in Munich peace is achieved. But will it last? The government is not sure. During the First World War over 1,400 civilians in England were killed in air attacks. In recent wars in Spain and Abyssinia entire towns have been destroyed by bombs. Despite air defences the government fears attacks on London could cause 600,000 deaths in the first week of war. There is no space to shelter everyone in London so the most vulnerable must be moved to safer parts of the country if war breaks out.

German Zeppelin

EARLY BOMBERS. Between 1914 and 1918 the Germans attacked England with Zeppelins and the more dangerous bi-plane Gotha bomber which could carry up to 12 bombs.

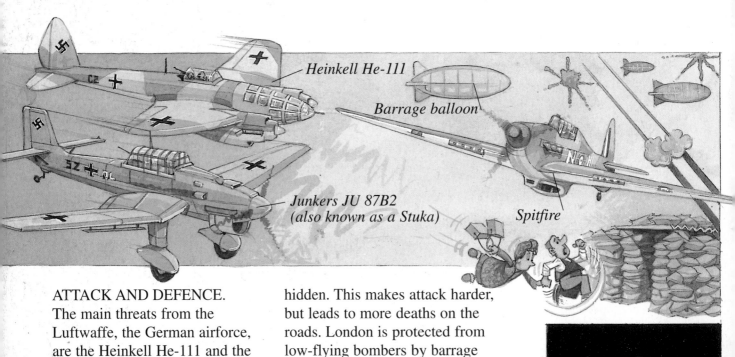

Heinkell He-111

Barrage balloon

Junkers JU 87B2 (also known as a Stuka)

Spitfire

Oo, it's dark!

ATTACK AND DEFENCE. The main threats from the Luftwaffe, the German airforce, are the Heinkell He-111 and the Stuka Dive Bomber. The Stuka releases its bomb as it nose-dives towards its target on the ground. At night all lights are turned off or hidden. This makes attack harder, but leads to more deaths on the roads. London is protected from low-flying bombers by barrage balloons, Spitfire and Hurricane fighters and anti-aircraft guns. Even so, air-raid shelters are the safest places during an attack.

War is declared

"...now at war..."

The government's fears are right. At 11.15 am on Sunday 3rd September, 1939, the Prime Minister announces on the radio that Britain is at war with Germany. Adolf Hitler has invaded Poland and Britain will help defend the country. Your parents look very worried, your dad will have to join the armed forces and your brother the Air Raid Precautions (ARP) services. Suddenly, there's a strange wail. It's the air-raid siren and you all rush into the nearby underground station, grabbing some belongings and your gas mask as you go. But it's a false alarm. In the shelter you hear your parents discussing whether you should join the 3.5 million children who have already been moved from London.

The Armed Services

Conscripts are asked if they want to be in the Army, the Royal Navy or the Royal Air Force, formed only 21 years earlier. Older and younger men were expected to join their local ARP branch as air-raid wardens (right).

Army

Navy

Air force

Put that light out!

Air-raid warden

Getting ready to go

Your parents have decided to send you away. Many mums are going too, but yours has decided to stay and work at the munitions factory in Woolwich. You have been sent a list of things to take, but your family can't afford many of them. When you get to the railway station you stay close to your school friends. You're all wearing labels with your names on. Teachers struggle to organise you, while many mums, including yours, are very upset. It's the first time you've been separated from your family, but mum says you'll be back soon.

WHAT YOU WILL NEED.

The government advises each parent to send their child away with: a gas mask, food for 24 hours, warm clothing, night clothes, clean underwear, plimsolls, a toothbrush, soap and a towel, a hairbrush and a warm coat. Your coat has been your brother's, and it was secondhand when mum bought it for him, so it isn't very warm.

Schoolchild

WHO'S LEAVING?
As well as schoolchildren, expectant mothers, invalids, the elderly and teachers were all evacuated from Britain's cities.

It'll all be over by Christmas.

Teacher

Expectant mother

Elderly

Invalid

Handy hint

You probably don't have a suitcase, so pack your things in a pillowcase and make sure it is labelled.

Has anyone seen Jones?

Address ...58 Ryshloke Rd
FOOD OFFICE CODE No.

The journey

Your journey has started and you're too nervous to settle down and enjoy the adventure. You are worried because it's your first trip on a steam train. You share your comics with two boys. It's scary when the train goes into a long tunnel and everyone screams. A boy is sick over your friend when he eats all his dinner and everyone else's sweets. You talk about the children who are being sent to America, Australia and Canada. You don't know where you're going.

Map of United Kingdom

Edinburgh
Glasgow
Newcastle
Leeds
Liverpool
Manchester
Birmingham
London
Portsmouth

WHERE ARE YOU GOING? The map (left) shows the main cities at risk of attack. Two hundred and forty thousand children are evacuated from London itself. Rural communities like Lancashire and Sussex received the highest number of evacuees.

Overseas destinations for some evacuees

Canada
USA
UK
Australia

U-boat

Torpedo

There's danger going overseas. On its way to Canada a U-boat sinks a ship called *City of Benares*: 256 people die – 77 of them children

Name ...THOMPSON
Other Names ...R.E.H

Arrival

Billeting Officer

You've arrived – you're in the village school at a place in Sussex. You're tired, hungry and scared because your friends have been left at other villages. A smartly dressed lady says she is the Billeting Officer and will find you a new home. Some of the other children have had their heads shaved to get rid of head lice. You all stand against a wall while grown-ups stare at you. The Billeting Officer says they will get some money for looking after a child. Every so often a child is picked and taken away. Will anyone ever pick you?

16

BROTHERS AND SISTERS are often separated. Many families only have room for one child.

OLDER BOYS are chosen first. They can work on the farms.

Handy hint

Try to tidy yourself up and smile. Clean and pretty girls are likely to be chosen quickly.

I'll take that one!

Your new home

ou are chosen by a smartly dressed lady who lives in a very grand house. Everything is huge, except your room. You soon realise she just wants another servant. You have to work hard, scrubbing and washing. As you read a letter from home you feel lonely – it'll be another month before your mother can visit, but at least your dad is still safe in England. Some of your friends have been taken home by their parents and others have run away back to London.

Scrub harder! You've missed a stain!

TAKEN BACK. Your host decides to return you to the Billeting Officer. Children were returned for various reasons, including being scruffy, wetting the bed and having head lice.

Handy hint

Learn to use cutlery properly. You will be scolded if you use your fingers.

Head lice

Scruffy

Bed-wetting

THE HOME GUARD. Men between 40 and 65 join the Local Defence Volunteers or 'Home Guard'. Many have fought against Germany in the First World War. Uniforms and rifles are scarce, so they use farm and garden tools as weapons.

YOUR NEW FAMILY. The Billeting Officer asks another couple to have you. They run the village shop and want you to help them. They seem nicer than the last lady. The husband is in the Home Guard.

19

Life in the country

Chomp, chomp...

You start to enjoy your new life. You attend the village school. You go for walks in the countryside but your shoes are worn out and your dresses torn. Your new family won't buy you any more and your mother has written to say she can't afford to send any money. The local children bully you, they laugh at the way you talk and call you and the other evacuees 'vaccies'. In the spring you are very homesick. Your parents visit you but don't take you home. London has not been attacked yet, but France has been defeated and British soldiers have had to be rescued from the beaches of Dunkirk.

Pooh! I can smell a vaccie.

SUMMER IN THE COUNTRY.
You have fresh strawberries covered in fresh cream for the first time! You see real cows and sheep and learn where milk comes from.

WINTER IN THE COUNTRY.
The autumn was mild, but your coat and shoes are old and will not keep you warm in the winter snow.

So that's why boys call milk cows' pee!

Doing your bit

If England is to win the war everyone must help, including you. Food is in short supply because German U-boats are sinking the ships bringing it from America. The government launches a 'Dig for Victory' campaign and you help to grow vegetables and pick fruit for jam. Food and clothes are rationed, but there are still sweets. The new plain chocolate bars are nice, but very small. The village shop sells 'ration bags' of sweets, nuts and popcorn. You have to drink cod liver oil! Now you are a Girl Guide you help collect aluminium saucepans to make Spitfires. But in September 1940 the German bombing of London, called the Blitz, begins. You worry about your parents.

FOOD FOR A WEEK. In May 1941 one adult's weekly ration of food included 225 g of jam, 1.7 litres of milk, 170 g butter, 30 g cheese, 225 g of sugar, 115 g of bacon, 55 g of tea, an egg and one shilling's worth of meat.

RATION BOOKS. Everyone has one for food and clothes: green books for babies, blue for children, yellow for adults. In the books are sheets of points to exchange for meat, butter, etc.

Oooh! I'd love some Spam.

Spam!

He's got Spam.

Back home at last

I t is now late 1942 and at last you can go home. Britain's forces are doing well. The speeches of Winston Churchill, the new Prime Minister, have raised morale. The RAF have defeated Germany in the air and the Americans and Russians are now fighting Germany too. But you find much of your street, and your home, was destroyed in the Blitz. You have to live with an aunt – she has a Morrison Shelter so you can stay indoors during night raids. You play in the streets and look for trophies, like pieces of parachute silk. It is highly prized for making underwear.

Morrison shelter

MORRISON SHELTERS. These indoor shelters were named after Herbert Morrison, the Minister of Home Defence. They could be used as tables during the day.

Winston Churchill

THE BATTLE OF BRITAIN. In the summer of 1940 Hitler ordered his air force to destroy the RAF before he invaded Britain. By the end of September the RAF had won.

Going away again?

It is 1944 and London is under attack again. Adolf Hitler has a new weapon – the 'Flying Bomb'. These V-rockets are fired from France to fall on London. The Germans fire about 100 a day and they have killed many people. You spend more time in the deep underground shelters and have school lessons in them too.

A new wave of evacuation has begun but your mum doesn't want you to go away again. After D-Day the attacks become less frequent as the rocket launch sites are captured. When it is safe you go to the cinema to see films, cartoons and the newsreels showing the Allied army freeing France and moving east towards Germany.

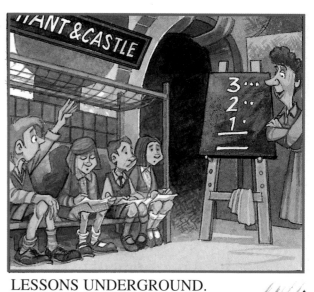

LESSONS UNDERGROUND.
Lessons go on in the shelters, which are also fitted with bunks for sitting and sleeping.

D-DAY, 1944.
On 6th June, 1944 almost two million Allied soldiers landed on the Normandy beaches on the French coast to drive the Germans out of France.

Handy hint

Join the school's rocket-watching rota. If one comes, ring the bell to get everyone to the shelters.

Here comes another!

Peace!

I t is 8th May, 1945 and VE (Victory in Europe) Day. Germany has surrendered and you and your family have survived. You listen to Winston Churchill declaring the end of war in Europe. He finishes with the words 'Onward the cause of freedom and long live the King'. Your dad will be coming back from service in Italy. You go to a street party and eat jelly and toffees. But life will not get better quickly. It will be years before all the buildings are repaired. The winter of 1946 will be the coldest of the century and the River Thames will freeze. But you will be with your family and the next government will try to solve the problems of poverty and ill-health with the new welfare state.

Chomp...

BLITZ VICTIM.
It will take a long time for many victims of the Blitz to recover from their injuries.

Bed sheet tablecloth

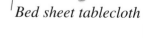

Handy hint

To brighten up your street party use old decorations from the parties that were held for King George VI's coronation in 1936.

Splat!

Thank God that's over – I can't face another air raid!

Hey! That's mine!

ATOM BOMBS. Japan surrendered on 15th August after the Americans dropped atomic bombs on the towns of Hiroshima and Nagasaki. The Second World War was over.

Glossary

Allied Where one country agrees to help defend and fight with another country against a common enemy.

Appeasement The British government's policy of giving in to Hitler's demands in the 1930s in the hope that it would prevent war.

ARP services Air Raid Precautions services. An organisation which helped people during air raids.

Atomic bomb An extremely powerful explosive bomb. One atomic bomb could destroy an entire city.

Barrage balloons Large gas-filled balloons flown over London. Designed to stop the German bombers flying low over the city.

Billeting Officer The person responsible for finding homes and guardians for evacuees in each village or town.

Blitz Short for the German 'blitzkrieg' or lightning war. The name given to the bombing of British cities by the German air force during the Second World War.

Conscript Someone who is forced to join the armed forces. During the war, this applied to all British men aged between 18 and 51.

Führer German for 'Leader' and the title Adolf Hitler gave himself in 1934 to show he was the one ruler of Germany.

Girl Guides Organisation for young girls who wanted to be active outdoors and help other people. Boys could join the Scouts.

Home Guard The Local Defence Volunteers (LDV). Any man aged over

40 could volunteer to help defend Britain if Germany invaded.

Luftwaffe The German air force.

Munitions Bullets and shells for use in a gun.

RAF Britain's Royal Air Force.

Rationing A fixed allowance of food and clothing.

Respirators Special breathing equipment which can filter out any dangerous chemical gases and allow its wearer to breathe normally and safely.

Shilling A unit of money used in Britain before 1971. There were 20 shillings in an old pound.

Spitfire One of the RAF's single-seat air defence fighters.

U-Boat A German submarine.

V-Rockets German unmanned flying bombs, sometimes nicknamed 'doodlebugs'.

Welfare State The new British Government in 1945 set up a system to provide free health care to all and education to all children.

Zeppelin An early type of German bomber. It was a large (180 metres long) hydrogen gas-filled balloon with a motor.

Index